CONFESSIONS
of Poetry

AF423115

Arz

First Published in March 2023

ISBN: 978-93-5741-058-8

BLUEROSE PUBLISHERS

www.BlueRoseONE.com

info@bluerosepublishers.com

+91 8882 898 898

Cover Design:

Arz

Typographic Design:

Hemlata

Distributed by: BlueRose, Amazon, Flipkart

Dedicated to my sunshine

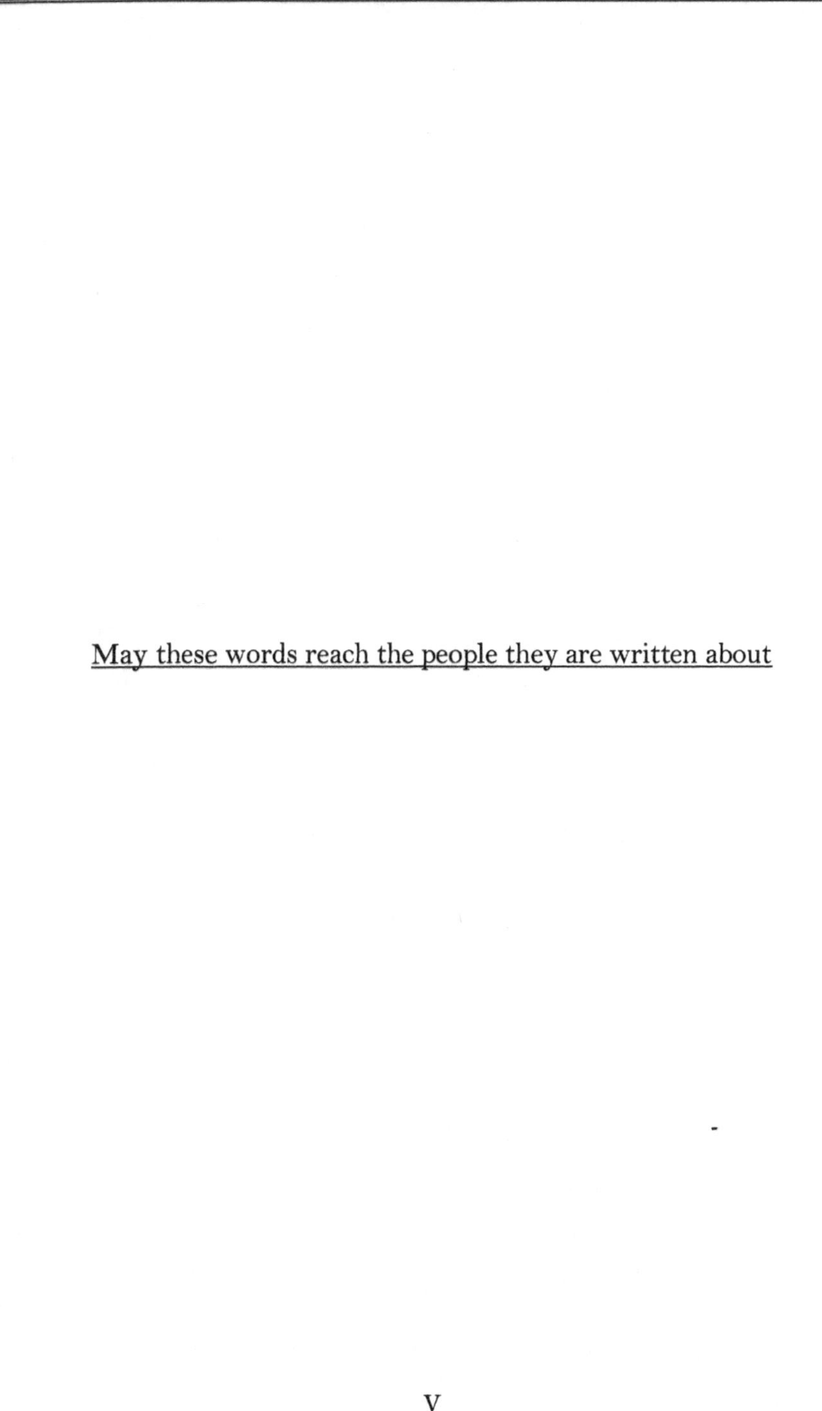

<u>May these words reach the people they are written about</u>

Hello Dear Reader,

Here's a small note before you start.

At first, I wanted to name this book <u>'Confessions by poetry'</u> but instead of 'By' I changed it to 'of'. The meaning behind this title is that poetry is a feeling or a mixture of various feelings and this is what depicts in this book a <u>mixture of various emotions.</u> The way I went through different emotions while writing these poetry I want every person who is reading this to feel that.

The beauty of poetry is that it makes people feel something.

I hope you have a great day!
Thank you,
ITsArz

About the Author

ITsArz is a pen name for Arz. She is a 19-year-old law student. She has been writing poetry for years and has published over 20+ poems in different anthologies by her pen name. This is her first book with her original name.

When she is not writing or reading, she likes to travel, explore and create new memories. She is also fond of music, art, and making people smile.

Keep in touch with Arz via the web:

Twitter: https://twitter.com/i_t_s_a_r_z/
Instagram: https://www.instagram.com/i_t_s_a_r_z/

Mail:authorarz@gmail.com

Thank you Mom for your support.
And also a big thanks to all the people who encouraged me,
inspired me and motivated me.

A Thousand Words Burning Inside Me
Will Come Out in An Epiphany
A Rhapsody, Some Little Beats of a Memory.

Hopeless Romantic
Delicacy Of Heart
Mind So Sore
At Night I'm At The Shore.

Contents

Chapter Three: Found A Paradise, Somehow

Chapter Four: Ending with The Finest Words

Chapter One

Those Were the Dark Nights in The Town

A Part of Me Demise That Day.

How do you define the dark ?
It lives inside you
I am your dark
Do you define me ?
Read me
Write me
Or just Feel me .

Mirror Mirror on the Wall

I looked in the mirror on the wall
And asked,
Who is the broken from us all
And it looked me back
And said,
The one who is asking the question
Would know it all

Sometimes the ground starts to shake
With the thunder in my brain
It bothers me from the inside
But how to show it from the outside

A deadly sin is calling my name;
I am listening with cold feet
A dumb brain
A foggy vision
And a vicious smile.

Shower Thoughts

Drowning in the sky
Flying underwater
Dying to feel a little
Wanting to feel a little less

A mess of brains
The art of hearts
It just beats a little more
To be a little less orphan of the world

The touch of the skin
The burn in the brain
The water in the eyes
And all these shower thoughts in my head.

Dark Thoughts

The dark is here
And I'm in it
The never-ending emotion of the depiction
Between a sentimental heart and a skeptical mind.

The balance between life, floral happiness,
Things don't make sense, Is when I feel alive;
Something is there
That is calling to be felt
And act,
Maybe, to find some sense
But not here.

The lost to be found, Where to begin?
The end is near, Where to see?
The look in your eyes, Where have I been?

With the Waves

Let me tell you a story
Which is much of a vision
I dreamt of drowning
And here I am, living in the water

I look through these delicate waves
And I see them gazing at me
I did wondered
What do they see in me?
Life, maybe
Although they went flowing by
But also took me with the waves.

Time to Dissolve in the Sky

I'm sitting tonight on the floor
Looking at the moon
It is full tonight;
I wish I was too
It's just us tonight
The moon, me, and the dark

I wanna write
But, I feel like running
I wonder, how this brain is so big
And carries nothing inside

The moon is staring tonight
Do I look different?
Am I something else?
Am I something you never thought I was?

I can't understand, But here I am
Next to you
The sky is all mine
And as my time will come
I surely will dissolve in it.

These Feelings of Yours

I don't know "how to speak?"
Act or feel.
These feelings of this enormous heart

These feelings kills me to death
Wakes me alive
But it never comes closer to me
Figuring them out alive

This does scares me
Sometimes I even breathe on these feels
Maybe they feed on me.

This spectacle brain can understand this gigantic universe,
but, not a beating heart of its own.

Is this how it should be like?
Or am I just a fool
Who only knows how to pick a pen

Maybe it is gonna be alright
At least these feelings are not mine
They are belonging of someone else
Who left it in a mess for me
And this is how it comes out all alive
Not for me
But for someone else
To understand.

Dry Heart

There's no moon today
Is this another story repeating
Is it us
Or just me.

Look above,
The sky's clear today;
I'm killing
The weather today;
Somebody is hurting in the wind,
I'm listening today;

I'm dancing,
With my beloved dark
On the rusty floor today;
With all the water in my sky,
My eyes feel numb
Moreover,
My heart feels dry today.

Why?

You wanted it
But didn't get it
You needed it
But didn't accept it
It's the incomplete sense of actions
That's left, all now
It's all mindless, senseless, breathless
Soul craving
Deprived disease
That am I
So what it is like to be left in the middle
Is the question I never asked
Why?

I Have A Fever

My sky is crashing down
I have a fever
I have been in love
But, it brings up my tears
My eyes are open
But I feel closed inside
Why does this feeling stay?
Is the question I never asked, why?
An emotionally recked heartbeat
Is beating me now
The pain is not new
But the flavor is somehow
 Do I believe in the past?
Or do I live in it
Even if I don't
I tears sure do have a past to tell now
My sky was open before, But it is closed now
Because it is crashing down at my doorstep
A day
Everyday.

I'll Be Here

Nobody knows
Who I am?
Where I am going?
I see the path
Filled with smoke and cold around
I get the idea of running
But my brain prefers to fly.
Is different a choice?
Or a place.
The place is me
So if I didn't go too far
I'll always have somewhere to be.

All the colors are mixed into one
And I have to pick one
So I prefer the rainbow
And I like the cold
Even if my feet are cold.

These long nights are my daydreams
These streets are my shine
The blue is mine
The sky is peace
And now, let me go

To discover, what is missing?
And is still here
Even if it doesn't make sense
I'll still be here.

Is It Fine?

Is it fine to be lost, and still wander?
Being highly adored by the sky, still feel unlovable

For a delicate heart
A hug indeed
A kiss of unspoken words
Was like being adored by the eyes of the brown.

A laugh in misery
A cry in love
Still smiling through it all
My heart will tell you a lot.

A Way

The sun is up there
And I am in the shallow
The end is here, behind my back
The dive and ride
Dark and blue
All the colors through the grey spectrum
Washes away in the blue ;
It's overcrowded, turn the station
The houses at the end keep calling me home
The lavender essence, drown me in it

I am driving, too far
Too close to the end line
But the line is breaking
The more I drive
The more it goes away
So far away
And I can't find the way.

I Left

I suppose, I dropped those scars on the floor as I walked away

I suppose, the blood dried on the walls as I locked the place

The tears are already buried in the grave

It felt like losing my heartbeat while being alive

Like drowning underwater looking for a last breath

A reason to live

Cause being alive isn't enough

Taking 20,000 breaths wasn't easy

Falling from 50 feet above the ground is just a moment

But, standing there without falling is something different

Standing at the height of 23,000 feet, still felt like my soul was buried under the sea

The eyes were blue but grave

The hands were dry

Hair were rumbling with air

Every day, every minute, every second

I missed that place, and that's how I lived my part

A part of me demise that day.

The darkness has the tendency to take me away to a mysterious place I don't prefer to visit. It takes time but finding your place again after coming out of the dark is all the journey is about.

To find your place

Find your way

There will always be a place where you belong.

Chapter Two

Somewhere In The Wind,
I Belonged

It feels like the end
But it is barely the starting.

Love is a beautiful feeling
But where do you start?
Love yourself first
So that you can love the others
When the time comes.

Find yourself

Head feels heavy
Body feels light
Don't know if the time is lying
Is it the end or the start?

Losing someone isn't easy
But, losing yourself
Is a difficult path to walk

When the world fades away in front of your eyes
You look but you don't see
You say but don't talk
When you don't feel your heart beating
When you don't wander or think
It feels like deceasing
But it is the rebirth
Of the unknown.

Like a phoenix rising from the ashes
The dawn after dusk
Until you find yourself
Don't let your mind ripe your heart out.
Let your heart bleed
And cry
then let it fly

In the sky of rainbows.
Let it breathe in the fragrance of lilies
Make it feel like the rain
Don't let in drown
In someone else's vain.

When the day will come
You will shine again in the sun
Until then let yourself be a researcher
In finding your soul once again.

Women

She never wanted to be powerful
She never asked for rights
She admired the care
And accepted the pain

With just a carat of the ring
She sold herself
To the beloved

Everyday
Every word ever spoken had its consequences
Everywhere
She goes the silence was the only thing she received

Happiness was not to be presented
But to be brought
With a price
Of a soul

She stood in her house
Like in a battlefield
Without a sword
She lived her life
Without anyone knowing
She was dead inside.
She smiled with her eyes
While calming the bleeding heart Inside.

I wonder what a war
It would have been inside her
Or on the outside
She would have won
A battle of swords rather then the one inside
But she will grow
Find a way
To be her
Even if she don't even know her
She will built her
Better with the love
She holds in her .

Relive

What do you call a feeling you feel without a heart?
It's not a feeling it's pressure
That makes you believe that you can make it work
When there is not a single ray of hope
You try to look for the candle
That has already burnt your home.

In your home
You sit in the dark and wish for the light to come
You went to your funeral without a cry
Then looked into the mirror with a smile
When the morning came
Your eyes were still with blood
Your soul was so dry.

However
The water wasn't pale
And air never got wet
Stars always came with the evening sky
The sky was still blue
Crystal clear
Hope never got lost
It was just gone.

The Start

I am zoning out
I am flying,
Underwater
Down in the dept
I feel so lively
And filled
Like I am in a crystal ball
On display
I see glossy sunlight
Around me.

I feel blessed
I feel dark
I feel peace
I feel the end
I am motionless
Just flowing
Wherever I see space around.

No wandering
No finding
No enthusiasm
Just pale body
With a heart beating
Somewhere.

I could close my eyes
And let me go to the end of eternity,
But I feel blood running
I feel the bones cracking
I know the ache
I have been in that lane
It feels like the end
But it is barely the starting.

It's not over

She almost vanished
But then
She stopped near the barriers
And stood above them
She jumped into the cold water

In winter snow
 Let every inch of her body know
That it's not over
When the sun came
She walked in the sunshine like a golden flame
And then there was the shining again

When she ran between the trees
Into the wild
Let herself breath
She screamed inside
And shouted outside
All her fears died on that bare land
She buried them all with her rare hands.

You

There was someone who made you shed your tears
Also, there was someone who broke your soul
And the one who never cared for your heart
But there also was the one
Who never hurt you
Shielded you
Healed you
Loved you
Unconditionally
There was that person
And that person was you
Always
And one
You.

Her

That Monday morning
I looked at her
She was coming from the wind
With a flower in her hair
Braided and loosely tangled
Then her eyes locked on mine
Like my heart was full of wine
And my brain was filled with serotonin
She was an art
And I was an admirer
She was like a sweet wind that went right past me
And I was there
But I was not
Cause I was lost
In her magic.
The charm she holds
Is like a powerful magnet
And I was just a nickel
Without any movement
I got attached to her
Like a part of me was dropped accidentally
And she picked it up.

Nostalgia

A moment of feeling alive
A moment of feeling dead
A moment of laugh
A memory of love
The wonders with eyes
The thinkers with words
I was feeling nostalgic
So I just put in some words

Sometimes on a bare paper
Sometimes in an isolated mind
But to be nostalgic
And then acting normal is not alright
The first time felt like heaven's bliss
The second time made me feel at home
It was not a person
Not a place
Not a voice
Not a sound
Not even a glimpse
It was just something expressive
Something rock solid
That hit my soul.
How does one explain to be feeling nostalgic?
How does one know that it is a nostalgic feeling?

How to be sure
And not to be sure
How to explain, feel or understand?
It is so expressive and yet inexplicable

But also who are you to think
Or who am I to understand
We are all the same
A little lost in understanding
The complexity of everything

A moment of being nostalgic
It's just a moment of hope.

I Belonged

I am not a belonging
But
I belong to myself
My heart is always on my sleeves
But
I keep them fold
I feel a little under the weather
But still,
I put myself together
I am an open book
But
My book is not complete.

I adore the music
Because
It adores me,
I am fond of the moon
Because
It has seen me,
I listen to the rain
Because
It completes my silence.
The sun makes me glow
The wind makes me smile
I crawl into the arms of nature
Because
It comforts me uptight.

From dawn to dark
I lookup
So I won't let myself down,
Its never blank
Its always blue, black, and golden
Like the shades of the eyes
Or maybe it is the eyes
That has seen me
As the years passed by,
Through the windows
I sit by.

It is the comfort of clouds
That makes me feel
Welcome
like a home
I never owned
But still, I belonged
Here
There
Somewhere
Between the sky and the ocean.

The hope is never lost
It was just gone
And with time
I found it again
It was just a way
I found me again .

Chapter Three

Found A Paradise, Somehow

The wind around me
brings me close to you

A feeling,
That would have been found in many wonders
But rather, I found it in one heart.

Mine

Laying on the bed of roses
Eyes never blinking
Wearing winter clothes
But, feeling naked in each other eyes

It is real, isn't it
Losing your soul
Without losing your body
While finding it in someone's eyes
Without being touched
It is a dream, isn't it

I don't know, which way to go
The only place I know is in his arms
A cold body confiding in a warm embrace
That's where I found a home
That's where my heart stops shouting
Because mine met his
My heart is not mine anymore
And I am in euphoria
I don't wanna be anywhere else, but here
In the moment of eternity
With his heart
Calling mine.

The Foolish of Fools

I'm wearing red
A romantic scenario in my head
The Friday specials, the foolish of fools

Those longing brown eyes
That sunflower-glowing smile
So, I'm gazing at it all in my daydreams
And at night.

Dumb

Hands holding
I like the way of talking
Heartbeats
The most calming
This was all we used to need.
Dumb conversations
Half words, half feels
Distraction yet solid.

Tired eyes,
Yet awake by each other
Placing hearts in one another
Feeling, only that feeling
That's all we need
The presence of each other
It's better for one another.

Thinking All About My Heart

A paradise
Hands in hands
Lips onto one another
Crushing into each other
Running time, racing heart
A standstill mind, rising high
In my head
I'm thinking about my heart.

Care

Caring for you
Like a winter moon
I shine bright
But still,wish you were by my side

The look in your eyes
Gives me paradise
I melt in your arms
The way my heart slide

Being close to you
Gives me a kind sight
Hope you'll kiss my hand
Next time you'll sit by my side.

Cold

The moon is mine tonight
Just like you were once that night
My beloved,
My heart is deprived
And the fire in it is dying

The cold is getting to me now
Cause the weather is so down
So pull me up in your arms
Warm my heart in yours

Let me breathe, for this minute
Then I'll go back to the moon for the night.

More Than Enough

You play a song out of love
I read some lyrics at the end
To capture the words

The silent night, that came
With your lips touching mine
The delicate vein in the hand
And then I felt
You, on my neck

A soft touch with a little tease of brown eyes
I wish for only good luck
On our side

Something just mine
Something so good
I just got a new flavor
With a mirror in front
Your arms around me
Is more than enough
How do I tell you all this?
Without knowing some words.

Perfectly Fine

Just a touch of him
And I feel fine
The world makes me foolish
But he still knows to love me right

It feels too strong at times
To be handled by a little heart
However, sitting next to him
Feels alright

My mind is insane at times
Then he is my brain
With not much
But little love from him
Keeps me perfectly fine.

Built with Me

Built with me, drive with me
Then there will be something
Rather than nothing
Be colorful
Paint me around your world
Fly with me in the sky I own
Dive right into the sea, swim all the way
Let this world be a little easy while being with me.

Be Mine?

Can you be my fever?
Can I be your muse?
Can you be a little more?
So that I can be a little less

Will a kiss be fine?
Your hands in mine
Is the wind around us alright?

What do I look like from your eyes?
Did you hear my heart say your name?
So now with all the feelings
Can I ask you to be mine?

Disappear

Lips on my neck
The world has gone by
Something with his touch
That keeps my moans right
The kiss with a taste
I'll never get tired by
We disappear in each other
Until the time is running by.

Drown in Those Eyes

Waking up and seeing your eyes
Are the mornings, I prescribe
Sunlight touching our bodies
While we lay in silence and roses
 Mind so calm cause I drown in those eyes

A kiss with a touch of my taste
Your hands drew maps on the skin
Where you travel every night
Love that we discovered
On the ground of peace
Forever doesn't seem so difficult
When you have days like these.

To You

I smiled
When I felt that heart beside me
When it touched me
A spark went through my brain

The feeling I speak about,
Would have been found in many wonders
But rather, I found it in one heart

I am running
Rather not with you
But, somehow around you
And I am trying
To not get lost
But it feels too euphoric, not to.

So long, as it sails
I am home
I feel an emotion
And a heart
That brings me home
To you.

Close to You

All the atoms together
Binding in one motion
To bring me close to my heart
To you.
The wind is here
And there,
It drives me away
It fades me out
But it brings me close to you.

Two Hearts

The
Two hearts burning
Around the corner
Leaves falling from the trees
Around two joined bodies
The deeper and deeper
They fall
The more and more they fly
To ignite in the sky.

An emotion
A feeling
A home
Essence of my heart
On this paper
Just feels right

How was the feeling ?

Like I was a bird and the sky was all mine

It was a delightful feeling.

Chapter Four

Ending with The Finest Words

Your love didn't break me
It saved me
From me

These words

They are fine in there own light

They are not together

But still make sense with one another.

The Wildflower

The wildflower burning down the lane
Yet blossoming through the wind
The midnight calls upon us, yet
I still sit by the same lane
The train came and went
I never left, the way
All day, all say
Words of mind, games of hearts
Below the fire, you'll find me in the dark
Laying with my heart, the wind passes by
Looks like a dream, all that I didn't say
I waved, and the shore went away
I played, the song breaks away
I stayed, the tracks blocks my way
I said I didn't say the same
I choked away
No other games I played on my way.

Now

I'm calling for you now
I'm calling for poetry
Do come to me now
Bring the peace of tray with you

The time has long gone now
The after-hours are over
The sun is there
But the shine of the moon is gone
Who is looking at it all?'
Am I even a person?
Or just in my brain?

I keep on moving with the thoughts
In the surroundings,
To see destiny,
To somewhere,
But where does this path goes
How to stay?
Just where I am now.

On the Inner Side

People are affected by other people
Here I am in the effect of myself
It's my conflicts
That I stand on the ground.

I drown in the misery
With a mask on my face
I mourn with disappear
Restructured deep inside there is a place.

I see the pain of others
With a glance of an eye
While I drown myself
Down inside.

Quite defeated
I win at life
And it all glows outside
While I burn on the inner side.

all well on the outside

Your Mystery

She is a mystery

A muse

Read her through and you will flew

A brain more of a maze

A heart running a race

She is destined to see waves

A smile of a haze

Shine, as she behaves

The golden glow of her skin

Touches your soul from within

As the autumn leaves

Drops from these trees.

Swim

The hands start to shake
Freezing in the wind
These blackout days
All beneath my own grave
I only shine with grace.

Something inside breaks away
The blood dried, and I left my place
Blue is the new grey
Calling for the sunlight and I see no rain
The crew sinks yet I swim at my wave.

Emotions

Emotions, here
Too much, too many
I am better being alone
Rather, rapid on the streets
My sky goes smooth
From the words, I love to hear
Emotions, here
Too much, too many
I hide a part of me
Emotions bring it out, all here.

Heal

Life is wired, a little delusional
Perhaps, I feel my brain in my heart sometimes
Play the keyboard and the music comes out alive
I am still a human then why should I stay blind?
Behind the curtain
Below the wind and in the dark
When I have fire in my hand,
It heals every wound that ever found me.

Bring back the shine

What did I see in these clouds?
What did I wonder?
Away from them and I'll crumble.

The orange sunset hiding in these clouds
Behind the wind
I see, two people joining with all this.

The soft whistle
By someone
And I'm gone forever
In these clouds.

Like a sweet chocolate jar
The sky is fading away
Taking me with it.

Find me around this wind
Somewhere in the clouds
In there blue
With my shine back in its time.

Painting of my heart

Finding decency in chaos
Unraveling the mysteries of calm
Looking in the blue
So there's the ocean where I didn't drown.

Looking back at past
All words are around
The merry all-day round
Where now I couldn't see
Show me around.

Finding all of it now
The painting of my heart
I drew it with my past.

Built it

Hands in hands
So it's a romance
Love is a definition
So uncomplicated
All the lies in the mind
We tell to calm ourselves
Humans don't belong anywhere
But still built a house in hearts somewhere.

Secure Heart

I see these days
So history repeats
I might have left
But I would have stayed

I left my heart here
Keep it, secure
These days are rusted
It might get tinted on the floor

People change, but the story is still the same
How did this story play?
And my heart stayed the same.

Your Love

Love doesn't break you

It saves you

From the darkness boiling inside you

If you find it keep it

As long as it lasts

Its taste will capture the insight of you

You might not even remember

It doesn't bring out the best

But it saves you from the last

Keep it as a power, right inside your heart

- close to my heart

Great are the words that hold a tendency to tell a story

A mystery is a poetry that tells so much

In so little

It is the mind which sees it all and still says nothing, but rather just feels.

Confession

That lives in your heart

Dives In your mind

Hides in the sky

Flows in the sea

And a paper that holds it at night.

THANK YOU